RETURN OF THE RED NOSE JOKE BOOK

Compiled and edited by Rod Green

First published in the UK 1991
by BOXTREE LIMITED, 36 Tavistock Street, London WC2E 7PB

1 3 5 7 9 10 8 6 4 2

Designed by Design 23
Illustrations by Rowan Barnes-Murphy, Martin Shovel,
Paul Demeyer, Robin Kingsland, Rod Green

Cartoons from The Viz Book Of Crap Jokes with kind permission
of Viz comic

Special thanks to the children of Leverhulme Memorial School, Harris

Printed in England by Lawrence Allen, Weston-super-Mare

British Library Cataloguing in Publication Data
Comic relief - the stonker: return of the red nose joke book.
1. English prose : Humorous prose
828.9140

ISBN 1–85283–327–0

Dear Reeder

A man called Rod asked me if wood writ
sumething at the bigning of this buk. That was
very nice of im becos no one in my famlee ever
ownd a book befor. The onle tring we ever ownd
was a hameter and he got dun in by Mr Blackadder.

P.T.O →

Mr Blackadder tolled me this buk is ful of jokes that are abowt az funny as getting your bottom caut in a bacon slicer. I tolled him i thort he was rong and that the jokes are abowt as funny as some jokes that are very funny.

I also tolled him that I ~~thort thort~~ thort someone getting there ~~bottom~~ caut in a bacon slicer might be qite funy, in fakt. So he took me to a butcher shoppe with a bacon ~~slic~~ slicer in it and you know it turned out that he was right aftr all. It wasn't the slirtest bit funny.

Still — I hope you enjoi reeding the buk as much as I'm going to enjoi boiling it up with some vegtables and eeting it.

Yours with a very sore botom,
   Your umbel serve ant,

BALDRIK

Visiting your Aunty is exactly the time to crack some wicked gags about the rest of the family. No one else will be too pleased, but your dear old Aunty will laugh till she pops her corsets and reward you with mounds of her, ahem, "delicious" home made angel cakes.

Best give these to the dog.

Lucinda came home from her first riding lesson and told her dad that she'd had a great time.

". . .and after the lesson, they let me give the horse a drink."

"Aren't you supposed to say that you watered the horse?" said her father.

'Okay," said Lucinda, "I watered the horse. Now I'd better go and milk the cat."

RING-A-RING-A-NOSES

A boy came home after his first rugby game with a broken nose, a torn ear and three loose teeth, but he couldn't remember who they belonged to.

What did Dad say when he saw Daffy Duck pushing his face through the letter box?
"Oh, no! Not another bill!"

John came home from school one day with tears in his eyes.

"What's happened to you?" asked his mum.

"The other boys keep calling me a big cissy," sobbed John, "and hitting me!"

"Then you must hit them back," his mum advised.

"I can't ," sniffed John. "I might chip my nail varnish!"

A boy called round at his girlfriend's house one evening.

"Are we going out to eat?" asked the girl.

"Well, I thought we might just eat up the road," the boy replied.

"Oh, no," said the girl, "I don't think I'd like tarmac."

**What's that rustling noise outside the door?
Oh, it's just the paper boy.**

Here's one from Viz...

A man came home late from work one night to find his wife sitting waiting for him in the living room.

"What time do you call this to be coming home?" she yelled.

"Your tea is ruined so I threw it in the bin. I suppose you could take me out somewhere nice for dinner, but I'm not fit to be seen anywhere nice. You never buy me any new clothes. All I have to wear are the same old rags I've had for years. I'd like to be seen in something long and flowing for once!"

So he threw her in the river.

Wife - Darling, I think I can hear burglars downstairs. Are you awake?
Husband - Nope.

THE MAGNIFICENT SEVEN NOSES

"*YEEEEEUCH!!*" spluttered Father as the family sat down to tea. "This lettuce tastes awful. Are you sure you washed it, Lucy?" "Yes, Dad," answered his daughter, "but I couldn't get all the soap off!"

"Did your watch stop when it hit the floor, Dad? asked the little boy. "Of course it did!" snapped his father. "Did you think it would go straight through?"

Tailors Shop Joke

FRANKLY, I DON'T CARE IF YOU BUY ME OR NOT

THESE ARE A VERY CASUAL TROUSER SIR

...and here's another one from Viz...

Mum came rushing into the house one evening. "I've just had to walk for miles," she said, flopping down into an armchair. "How did you manage that?" asked Dad. "I punctured two tyres on the car." "I ran over a whisky bottle." she admitted. "That was daft," said Dad. "Didn't you see it?" "No," replied Mum, "the stupid old man had it in his coat pocket!"

"What happened to your grandad?" a little boy asked his friend.

"I heard he'd had an accident."

"He did," replied his friend. "He was in an explosion. He went looking for a gas leak with a lighted match."

"But he used to work for the gas board, didn't he?" said the boy. "I'd have thought that looking for a gas leak with a lighted match would be the last thing he would do."

"It was."

Aunty Annie came to visit and stayed quite late.

"Maybe you should spend the night here with us," Mum suggested.

"That's a good idea," agreed Aunty Annie and started to put her coat on.

"Aren't you going to sleep here?" asked Mum.

"Yes," said Aunty Annie, "but I'm just going to pop home for my nightie!"

My dad was called in to school to see the Headmaster about my little brother.

"What's he been up to then?" my dad asked as he entered the Headmaster's office.

"Well, I don't know how to tell you this," said the Headmaster, "but this morning we had to send your son home from school for having a wee in the swimming pool."

"Oh, really," said my dad. "Surely all little boys do the occasional wee in the swimming pool."

"Perhaps," replied the Headmaster, "but not from the top diving board!!"

Diana walked into the living room with her weekly pocket money stuffed into her mouth.

"Take that money out of your mouth!" said her mother. "It's probably covered in germs!"

"I doubt it," Diana replied. "Not even a germ could live on what you give me!"

ON THE WAY TO
AUNTY'S HOUSE

Little Charlie was walking along the street crying his eyes out.
"What's wrong with you, sonny?" asked an old woman.
"It's my birthday today," sobbed Charlie, "and all my best friends are at my house. They've all brought me lots of great presents and I've got a brand new bike to show them and we're having ice cream and jelly and cakes for tea!"
"That all sounds wonderful," said the old lady. "Why are you crying?"
"I can't find my way home!"

"Our dog," said the little girl, patting her faithful hound,
"is just like one of the family."
"Really?" said her friend. "Which one?"

Mary and Claire were staggering home from the shops laden with bags but without enough money left to pay their bus fares when they passed a signpost.
"Look at that," said Mary. "There's still two miles to go."
"Never mind," said Claire. "We're doing it together, so that's only a mile each!"

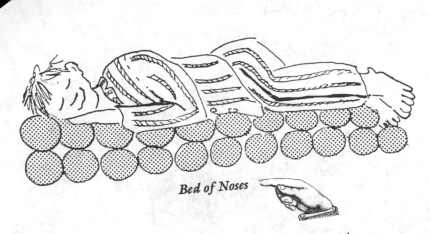

Bed of Noses

A beautiful girl went into a sweet shop and asked for a box of chocolates. "How much are they?" she enquired. "Since it's you," said the young man behind the counter, "just one kiss." "Okay," said the girl. "I'll send my grandad round to pay you this afternoon!"

When they were moving house, Dad got stuck on the stairs with a large wardrobe. "This thing's heavier than I thought," puffed Dad as his young son looked on. "I asked Mum to help me. Do you know where she is?" "Yes," said the boy, "she's inside the wardrobe carrying all the clothes!"

GRANDMA, WHY DO YOU KEEP GRANDAD UNDER THE BED?
WELL, DEAR, I THINK HE'S JUST A LITTLE POTTY!

NOSES! GET YOUR OFFICIAL RED NOSES!

A little boy had been sent off to a birthday party all dressed up in his best clothes and clutching a present for his school friend. His mother was a little surprised to see him coming up the garden path crying his eyes out just half an hour later.

"Er . . . how was the party?" his mother asked.

"I couldn't go," sniffed the youngster.

"Why not?" asked his mum.

"It says on the invitation 'From 3 till 6' and I'm 7!"

A man was astounded to walk into his son's bedroom and find him sitting playing chess with his dog.

"That's amazing!" said the man. "I never realised our dog was so clever!"

"He's not that smart," said the boy.

"He's only beaten me once today."

Out shopping with his mother one day, a small boy stopped at the bottom of an escalator and refused to budge.

"What's wrong?" asked his mother as the boy stood staring at the moving hand rail.

"Nothing," replied the boy. "I'm just waiting for my chewing gum to come round again."

The bin men were just about to climb into their lorry when a woman came running out of her house carrying a black bin liner.

"Am I too late for the rubbish?" called the woman.

"No," said the bin man, "help yourself!"

It was school report time and Mandy came home with her report card.
"Did you get the best marks in your class this year, Mandy?" asked her father.
"No, Dad," came the reply. "Did you get the best wages in your office this year?"

It was well past her bedtime, but little Nichola came running into the living room where her mum and dad were sitting.
"Mum, can I have a glass of water, please?" she asked.
"Another one, Nichola?" said her father, frowning.
"Yes," said her mother. "This must be about the sixth glass of water you've asked for."
"I know," said Nichola, "but my bedroom's on fire!"

A girl and her boyfriend had fallen out and he went round to her house the next evening to apologise, taking his dog with him for the walk.
"What are you doing with that pig?" asked the girl.
"It's not a pig, it's a dog," said the boy.
"I know," replied the girl. "It was the dog I was talking to!"

Granny - I'd like a fly spray, please.
Shopkeeper - I'm afraid we've none left. Have you tried Boots?
Granny - You must be joking! I want to spray the little devils, not kick them to death!

"MUM," SAID BRYAN, "PLASTIC BOTTLE, BREAD WRAPPER,
TIN CAN, OLD RAGS, CHOP BONES, EGG CARTON."
"SHUT UP, BRYAN," SAID HIS MUM.
"YOU'RE JUST TALKING RUBBISH AGAIN!"

Adrian was sent home from school after a school outing to the zoo with a note for his father asking poor old dad to go to see the Headmaster immediately. Adrian's dad trudged off down to the school and was invited into the Headmaster's office.

"Well," said Adrian's dad, "what's the little rascal been up to?"

"When we were at the zoo," said the Headmaster, gravely, "Adrian was caught feeding the ducks."

"So what's wrong with that?" asked Adrian's dad.

"He was feeding them to the tigers!!"

paul demeyer

Unless you want to be force-fed stale angel cakes until you weigh 73 stones, do not tell these jokes at your Aunty's.

Even the normally soppy old dog will turn on you, and at 73 stones, you won't be able to run all that fast.

The Vicar had come round to tea and was talking to Tommy and his mother about his daughter.

"Clara is ever so talented," he said. "She's only the same age as Tommy but I think she's already a good enough organist to start playing in church on Sundays."

"Really?" said Tommy's mother, sounding impressed.

"Do you have any special talents, Tommy?" asked the Vicar.

"I can do animal impressions," said Tommy. "This is an elephant."

"Er . . . I didn't hear any elephant noise there, Tommy," the Vicar confessed.

"Oh, I can't do the noises," said Tommy, "but just wait for the smell!!"

"Haven't you washed your face yet, Sam?" said his mother just before Aunty arrived for tea. "You won't get a kiss from your Aunty if you've got a dirty face."
"Yeah," said Sam. "That's what I thought!"

MUM! MUM! CAN I LICK THE BOWL?
NO, DEAR, JUST FLUSH IT LIKE EVERYONE ELSE!

"Mum, I'm fifteen now, so can I wear lipstick and eye shadow and blusher and jewellery and high heels?"
"No, Edward, you can not!"

"Mum," said the little boy, "why do you always cook breakfast in your dressing gown?"
"What's wrong with that?" asked his mother.
"Nothing," said the little boy, "but it might taste better if you cooked it in the frying pan!"

You might think that the doctor's waiting room is just the place to crack a few gags. After all, sick people need cheering up, right? WRONG!! Being thoroughly miserable is what people like MOST about being ill! Also, if you catch the doc in a bad mood and he or she hears you taking the mickey, there are lots of particularly nasty cures which can be prescribed, such as:

Boil on the neck -AMPUTATION!

Wart on the elbow -AMPUTATION!!

Runny bottom -AMPUTATION!!!

So beware at the doctor's. In fact, be VERY ware, otherwise your Mum might end up taking all your bits home in a carrier bag!

Doctor! Doctor! It's my nose!
Yes, I believe noses run in your family

"Miss Smith," said the doctor, "I think you've got acute appendicitis.

"Ooh," said the patient, "I'm glad you like it, doctor!"

Doctor! Doctor! I've got potatoes growing out of my ears!
That's incredible!
You're telling me! I planted carrots!

...and here's another one from Viz...

The Scarlet Pimplenose

...and here's another one from Viz...

Doctor! Doctor! You've got to help me!
Aren't you Count Dracula?
Yes, I am.
Well what's the problem?
It's my bat breath!

Doctor! Doctor! I think I'm a piece of toast!
Hmmm . . . I think you need buttering up a bit.

A toilet rushed into the doctor's surgery.
Doctor! Doctor! I feel all flushed!
Hmm . . . must be a chain reaction!

Doctor! Doctor! I think I'm a chocolate biscuit!
Well, come a little closer, I won't bite you.

**DOCTOR! DOCTOR! I THINK I'M MADE OF LIQUORICE!
WELL, IT TAKES ALL SORTS.**

NEW NOSES ON THE BLOCK

A doctor in a lunatic asylum walked past a well-known crazy who was dragging a mop behind him.

"Nice dog you've got there," said the doctor, deciding to humour the man.

"Don't be stupid!" replied the patient. "This isn't a dog, it's a mop."

"Oh . . . um, of course it is," said the embarrassed doctor, hurrying off along the corridor.

"Ha!" said the patient, turning to his mop. "Fooled him there, didn't we, Fido?"

ELF JOKE

SO LONG AS YOU'VE GOT YOUR ELF, THAT'S THE MAIN THING!

...and here's another one from Viz...

A woman walked into her doctor's surgery looking
very upset and wringing her hands with worry.
"*What seems to be the trouble?*" asked the doctor.
"*It's my son,*" wailed the woman. "*He plays at
pirates all the time, does wheelies on his bike,
throws mud at his friends, kicks his football
into the neighbours' garden and pings his
food around at the tea table.*"
"*Well, I don't really think there's too much
to worry about there,*" the doctor reassured her.
"*But I do worry, doctor,*" sobbed the woman,
"*and so does his wife!*"

Doctor! Doctor! I keep thinking there are two of me!
One at a time, please!

I NEVER WANT TO SEE YOU AGAIN!

DOCTOR. MY HAIR IS FALLING OUT.

I HATE YOU! I HATE YOU! I HATE YOU!

FSSS

Doctor! Doctor! I think I'm turning into a bridge!
What has come over you?
Three cars, two lorries and a motorbike!

"*Oooh! I'm in terrible pain, doctor,*" said the woman as she walked into the doctor's surgery. "*A wasp stung me on the finger.*"
"*Which one?*" asked the doctor.
"*I don't know,*" the woman replied. "*Wasps all look much the same to me.*"

Doctor! Doctor! My wife thinks she's an elevator!
Send her up to see me.
I can't! She doesn't stop on your floor!

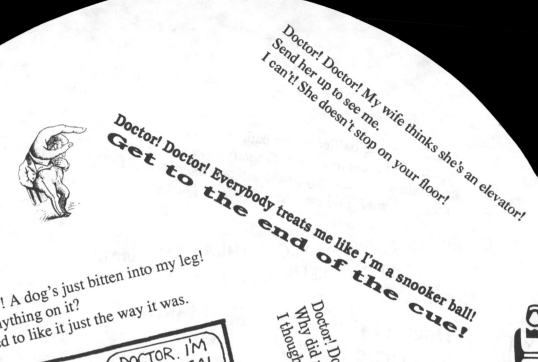

Doctor! Doctor! Everybody treats me like I'm a snooker ball!
Get to the end of the cue!

Doctor! Doctor! A dog's just bitten into my leg!
Did you put anything on it?
No. He seemed to like it just the way it was.

Doctor! Doctor! I've just swallowed fifteen ten pence pieces!
Why did you do that?
I thought the change would do me good!

DOCTOR. I'M IN A CRITICAL CONDITION!

I MEAN... JUST LOOK AT THIS CARPET. HOW PERFECTLY AWFUL!

CD

...and here's another one from Viz...

The doctor was baffled by his patient's mysterious illness. "I just can't seem to work out exactly what's wrong with you," he admitted. "*I can only imagine that it must be the drink.*" "*Okay, doctor*," said the man. "*I'll come back when you're sober.*"

DOCTOR! DOCTOR! EVERYBODY THINKS I'M A LIAR!
I DON'T BELIEVE YOU.

Doctor! Doctor! I keep thinking I'm invisible!
Who said that?

Doctor! Doctor! Why does no one like me?
You're stupid.
I want a second opinion!
Okay. You're ugly as well.

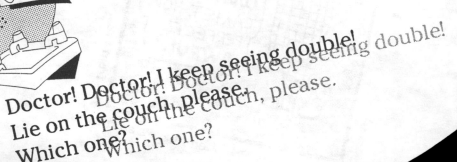

Doctor! Doctor! I keep seeing double!
Lie on the couch, please.
Which one?

Doctor! Doctor! I keep seeing double!
Lie on the couch, please.
Which one?

...and another one from Viz...

DOCTOR, IT'S MY HEART!

RR·CD 3·87

Doctor! Doctor! My husband's outside! He thinks he's a Range Rover!
Tell him to come in and see me. He can't! He's been wheelclamped!

Doctor! Doctor! I keep thinking I'm a bell!
Take some of these pills and if it doesn't clear up, give me a ring.

Doctor! Doctor! I feel like a racehorse!
I think you should stay in bed for a week or so.
I can't! I'm running at Cheltenham on Saturday!

...and here's another one from Viz...

"*My goodness!*" exclaimed the doctor as a patient walked in with a huge swollen nose.

"*What happened to you?*"

"*I bent down to smell a brose in my garden,*" replied the woman.

"*There's no B in rose,*" said the doctor.

"*There was in this one!*"

Doctor! Doctor! My son's just eaten our telephone!
What are you doing about it?
I'm phoning from the neighbours'!

Doctor! Doctor! I keep forgetting things!
How long has this been going on?
How long has what been going on?

"Oh, Doctor!" sighed the woman. "I don't know what's wrong with me these days. Most of the time, I just don't know where I am."
"Yes, I can see that, madam," replied the butcher.

Doctor! Doctor! How long can a person live without a brain?
I don't know. How old are you?

Doctor! Doctor! I tend to get fat in certain places. What should I do?
Stay away from those places.

Doctor! Doctor! I keep thinking I'm a bird.
Perch there and I'll tweet you in a minute.

DOCTOR. I THINK I'VE PICKED UP A BUG OF SOME SORT.

...and another one from Viz...

"Oh, doctor, you've got to help me!" wailed the woman. "My husband was sound asleep with his mouth wide open when the cat ran into the room chasing a mouse!"

"Why is that such a problem?" asked the doctor.

"Well, the mouse jumped straight into his mouth and disappeared down his throat!" explained the woman.

"In that case," advised the doctor. "Dangle some cheese in your husband's mouth to lure the mouse out."

"All right," said the woman, "and should I try dangling a fish there to get the cat out, too?"

Doctor! Doctor! I've just swallowed a bluebottle! Should I take anything for it?
No, let it starve!

Doctor! Doctor! Have you ever seen anything like this before.
Only once, and I had to pay an admission fee.

Two old friends met in the street.
"Where are you off to, George?" asked the first.
"I'm going to see the doctor, Stan," said the other. "I don't like the look of my wife."
"I think I'll come with you," said his friend. "I don't like the look of mine, either!"

Even if you are totally fearless and say things like "Ha! Amputated bottom? It's just a fleshwound. I've had worse than that playing dominoes!", you should never tell the following jokes anywhere near the doctor's surgery. Unless they've been on a course of laughing pills, no one at the doctor's will find these jokes in the least funny, and if you laugh at them, then we recommend that you see a doctor as quickly as possible since your sense of humour gland has obviously gone mental.

A man went to see his doctor one day.

"Doctor," he said. "I've got this terrible problem. I find that nowadays I prefer cats to dogs."

"There's nothing wrong with that," said the doctor. "In fact, I quite prefer cats to dogs myself."

"Really?" said the man. "How do you like yours? Fried or boiled?"

The zoo's always a good place for a few laughs.
Most of the animals like a bit of a giggle and the
hyenas will laugh at anything. Hamsters, on the
other hand, are a different kettle of piranhas altogether.
A hamster will go completely mental if you start slagging
him off. The little devil will tear the bars of his cage apart
and shoot up your trouser leg with his teeth bared before
you can say, "Only joking, Hammy!"

Two explorers were lost in the depths of the jungle in the middle of the night. "You know," whispered the first one, "we should be okay as long as the batteries in our torches hold out. I've heard that wild animals won't harm you if you're carrying a torch."

"That really depends," said the second one, "on how fast you carry it!"

 **WHAT'S GREEN AND HARD?**

What animal do you look like when you're taking a bath?
A little bear.

What do you get if you cross an elephant with a hedgehog? A two ton toilet brush!

What's the last thing to go through a fly's mind when it hits the front of your car? Its back legs!

THE NINE O'CLOCK NOSE

A FROG WITH A FLICK KNIFE!

WHY DO WILD DOGS HOWL IN THE DESERT?
BECAUSE THERE ARE NO TREES IN THE DESERT
- JUST CACTUS!

Having escaped from their field, two goats wandered around for a while until they found themselves in a rubbish dump. There were lots of interesting things lying around for them to eat and together they munched their way through a large book. Then one of the goats chewed up a long roll of film and swallowed it.

"What was the film like?" asked the other goat.

"Not bad," his friend replied, "but I preferred the book."

Sitting in the cinema one evening a woman was more than a little surprised to see a man walk in just before the film began with his pet crocodile at his side. The man and the crocodile settled down to watch the film, then during the interval, the crocodile got up to go to the toilet.

"I must say," the woman said to the man, "I'm surprised that an animal like that can appreciate this film."

"So am I," replied the man. "He hated the book!"

Why are parrots obviously much smarter than chickens? Well, you don't get Kentucky Fried Parrot, do you?

How do you make friends with a squirrel?
Stand under his tree acting crazy and the squirrel will take you for a nut.

What's the difference between a forged fiver and a crazy rabbit?
One is bad money and the other's a mad bunny!

What do Tarzan and the animals
sing at Christmas time?
Jungle Bells.

What do you get if you cross a cow with a kangaroo?
Nobody knows, but you'd have to milk it on a pogo stick!

How do you stop a skunk from smelling?
Cut its nose off!

What do you call a ferocious lion in a bad mood?

Sir!

Bear - How did your Full Moon Party go last night?
Wolf - Great! It was a howling success!

Troublesome Nose Hares

Two ducks were flying over their favourite pond when they
heard the sound of a hunter's gun and turned tail to flee.
"Quack! Quack!" said one, and the other one screamed,
"I'm goin' as quack as I can!"

A bumble bee flew frantically up the motorway with his back legs crossed, stopping briefly at each motorway service area as he passed it and muttering to himself:

"Drat - that's Shell! Drat - that's Esso! Drat - that's Texaco!"

"What's up with you?" asked a moth as he flew by.

"Isn't it obvious?" cried the bee. "I'm looking for a BP station!"

How do you stop a cockerel from waking you up at five o'clock on a Monday morning? Eat him on Sunday!

What's the difference between dogs and fleas? A dog can have fleas but a flea can't have dogs!

Why did no one care when the owl lost his voice? Well, he couldn't give a hoot, either!

Two cows were grazing in a field. "All this mad cow disease is very worrying isn't it?" said the first cow. "It doesn't bother me," said the other cow. "I'm a banana!"

What do you do with a sick sparrow? Get him tweetment!

A boy walked into a pet shop. "Got any puppies going cheap?" he asked. "No," said the shopkeeper, "all ours go woof!"

CHEAP

WOOF

Where do baby apes sleep? In apricots!

WHAT DO YOU CALL A SHEEP WITH NO LEGS? A CLOUD!

A man walked into a bar with his pet alligator. "Do you serve Americans in here?" he asked "Of course we do," replied the barman. "Okay," said the man. "I'll have a pint of lager and two Americans for my alligator!"

It was a quiet day in the clothes shop and the assistant there was rather surprised when his first customer walked in - a large grizzly bear.

"Er . . . what can I do for you, Mr Bear?" he asked.

"I'd like a fur coat, please," said the bear.

"What do you want a fur coat for?" asked the assistant.

"Well, I'd look a right wally in an anorak, wouldn't I ?" said the bear.

Eskinose

SPIDER JOKE

YOUR FLIES ARE UNDONE

?

At a local dog show one of the judges was puzzled by one of the entrants.
"This is a very strange breed, isn't it?" the judge said to the owner. "What is it?"
"It's a long tailed, short legged, long nosed retriever," said the proud owner,
"but some people call them crocodiles."

paul demeyer

No, even the
hyenas won't
laugh at these
and anyone who
has to put up
with you telling these gags is likely to let you take a
closer look at the lion's cage - like from the inside.
The inside of the lion that is . . . you'll be lunch!

Why did the fox cross the road?
To eat the *squashed* rabbit!

A bee and a butterfly settled on a flower together.
"Funny how your stripes look like a rugby jersey, isn't it?" said the butterfly.
"Actually, I used to play rugby," came the reply, "but I was only in the B team."

NOSE DIVE

Why can't leopards escape from zoos?
Because they're always spotted!

"Bzzz, I'm broke," said the bee to the rabbit.
"Can I sting you for a pound?"

How do you make your hamster a bit fatter?
Throw him off the roof and he'll go "PLUMP"!

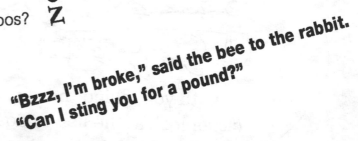

The only thing to remember about telling jokes at the breakfast/ lunch /tea/dinner /supper table is not to make anyone sitting opposite you laugh when they've got a half-chewed mouthful of tomatoey mush or curried gunge.

You'll never get the stains out of your t-shirt.

Waiter! Waiter! There's a little slug on my lettuce!
Just a minute, sir. I'll fetch you a bigger one.

Waiter! Waiter! What's this fly doing in my ice cream?
Er . . . learning to ski?

Waiter! Waiter! This food isn't fit for a pig!
I'll take it back and find you some that is, sir.

BOGEY MAN

At a dinner party in the British Embassy, an Italian General sat opposite the British Ambassador dressed in an impressive uniform decorated with an even more impressive display of medals.

"I say," said the Ambassador to his aide. "What did he get all those for?"

"About four quid probably!" the aid replied.

Waiter! Waiter! I've found a worm in my spaghetti!
Well, that's better than finding half a worm!

Waiter!, Waiter! What's that slug
doing slithering through my salad?
About 2mph, sir.

Waiter! Waiter! Why is there a piece of rubber in my shepherd's pie?
Must have come off the shepherd's wellies, sir.

Waiter! Waiter! I didn't order this!
But you said you wanted to try something different!

WAITER! WAITER! IS THIS CHICKEN FRESH?
FRESH? IT JUST LAID AN EGG!

Waiter! Waiter! there's a fly paddling in my soup!
Don't you mean swimming, sir?
No, you didn't give me enough soup for that!

Waiter! Waiter! This lobster has only one claw!
Oh. It must have been in a fight, sir.
Well bring me the winner!

Waiter! Waiter! There's a fly in my mince!
Those little devils just don't care what they eat, do they?

Waiter! Waiter! There's a fly in my soup!
Oh, he's only little, he won't drink much.

Waiter! Waiter! How long will my sausage be?
About four inches, sir.

Waiter! Waiter! I can't eat this meat! Bring me the manager!
But you can't eat him either, sir!

Waiter! Waiter! You've got your thumb in my soup!
That's okay, sir, its not hot.

DONG!

Quasinoso

Snow White and
the Seven Noses

WAITER! WAITER! HAS THE CHEF GOT A PIG'S HEAD.
NO, SIR, IT'S JUST THE WAY HE PARTS HIS HAIR.

Waiter! Waiter! There's an awful film on my soup!
Well, what do you expect for 50p - Ghostbusters?

Waiter! Waiter! Why are these flies playing football in my saucer?
They have to practice, sir. They're playing in the cup next week!

ASTRONOSE

The restaurant manager called all his waiters
together to warn them about shady customers.
"Some of our diners," he said, "seem to look upon
our cutlery as a form of medicine."
"What do you mean?" asked one of the waiters.
"To be taken after meals!"

On no account ever tell these jokes during a meal. People will puke up all over the place and since it's your fault, you'll have to clear up the mess. You probably wouldn't be able to finish you pizza after all that, either.

Waiter! Waiter! You know the only difference between this pancake and a heap of fresh manure?
No, sir.
This pancake is cold!

Waiter! Waiter! Is this a slug in my steak pie?
I think you'll find it's fat, sir.
I know it is! It's eaten all the pastry!

A diner called the waiter over to complain about his food.
"Waiter," he said, "these peas are hard as rocks!"
The waiter picked up a fork and tried a few from the man's plate.
"They seem quite soft to me, sir," he said.
"So they should be" the man replied. "I've been chewing them for
the past twenty minutes!"

Waiter! Waiter! The beef surprise was lovely, but what's the surprise?
It was dog food, sir.

WAITER! WAITER! THIS BREAD IS LOVELY AND WARM.
SO IT SHOULD BE, SIR. THE CAT'S BEEN SLEEPING ON IT ALL AFTERNOON!

Well, you
don't really need to wait until Hallowe'en to
tell monster jokes – any old dark and stormy
night will do. Turn the lights down and gather round a
roaring log fire, or log-effect on the electric heater
if you're in a smokeless zone. Then mingle the most
gruesomest, grisliest ghost stories in among your
jokes. If there's a full moon, though, watch out for that
hairy kid from down the road. If he starts growling
and howling, leg it, quick!

All the little monsters were getting
ready for school.
"Mum, where's my schoolbag?"
"Mum, where's my breakfast?"
"Mum, where's my bus money?"
"Mum, where's my gym kit?"
"Mum, where's my slimey old socks?"
"Wait a minute!" cried their mother.
"I've only got three pairs of hands!"

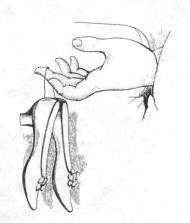

A monster's mum was out hanging up the washing in the
garden when she suddenly yelled at him:
"Quick! Get the knives and forks and some bread and
a few plates and take them next door!"
"Why, mum ?" asked the monster.
"The neighbour's just fallen into his barbecue!"

Why do witches fly on broomsticks?

Because a Hoover lea

Dracula went to the dentist and the dentist said :
"I don't think we've ever had a vampire in here before."
"Well," said Dracula, "fangs ain't what they used to be!"

Two monsters had just finished eating.
"I feel sick," said the first one.
"I know," said the other. "You can't keep a good man down!"

would never stretch far enough!

Two monster pals met up on their way to the school one morning.
"We had burglars last night," said the first one.
"Wow! That sounds exciting!" said his pal.
"Not really," said the first. "They don't taste nearly as good as teachers."

MUM, I HATE MY BIG BROTHER'S GUTS.
WELL, JUST LEAVE THEM AND EAT THE CHIPS.

"You're a bad piglet!" scolded
the mother pig. "If your father
could see you he would turn in his gravy!"

DAD

**What do you get if you cross a
monster with a boy scout?
A creature that frightens old ladies across the road.**

1st Monster - I'm thinking about becoming a vegetarian.
2nd Monster - Why's that then?
1st Monster - You can go off people you know!

Monster-You look like a million dollars.
Mrs Monster-You mean I look wonderful?
Monster-No, you're all green and wrinkly!

**WHAT'S A MONSTER'S FAVOURITE SNACK?
BEINGS ON TOAST!**

These jokes should never be told to your friends at Hallowe'en, on a dark and stormy night gathered round a roaring log effect electric heater, or at any other time for that matter. These jokes are liable to turn all your friends into a bunch of werewolves, vampires, swamp monsters and slime creatures just so they can get their own back on you. Of course, there's always the chance that your friends might already be a bunch of werewolves, vampires, swamp monsters and slime creatures just pretending to be normal. How can you tell? Well, slime creatures like dancing to Timmy Mallett records, but apart from that you've no way of knowing. Take great care...

paul demeyer

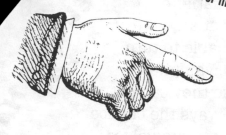

"I'd like a nice big Dog, please," said the monster, walking into the pet shop.
"This Alsatian is very nice," said the assistant, "and he's completely house trained."
"Never mind that," said the monster. "Will he taste good?"

How do you make a witch twitch?
Add a T.

How do you make a witch itch?
Drop the W.

What do you call a one-eyed dinosaur?
A Dyouthinkesawrus.

Little Monster-Daddy! Daddy! Granny's going out!
Big Monster-Pour some more paraffin on her, then!

Two monsters were at a party.
"Ooh!" said the first one to his pal. "That good looking ghoul over there just rolled his eyes at me."
"Well, don't just sit there, you fool," his friend replied.
"Pick 'em up and roll 'em back!"

Everybody tells jokes at school, but most
jokes are best kept for the playground. Teachers,
after all, are sensitive souls and easily upset -
especially P.E. teachers. If you get up the P.E. teacher's
nose he or she will think it's a brilliant laugh to give you so
much detention that you'll
be lucky to leave the class
in time to pick up
your pension.

Having talked for an hour about wild animals the teacher posed a question to one of her class. "Roger," she said "what would you do if you saw a ferocious tiger walking across the playground?" "I'd escape from it riding like the wind on a champion racehorse," Roger replied. "Oh, really?" said the teacher, "and where would you get a champion racehorse from?" "Same place you got the ferocious tiger, Miss!"

Teacher - What's your name, boy?
Pupil - Colin Brown.
Teacher - Say "Sir" when you talk to me!
Pupil - Okay. Sir Colin Brown!

Headmaster - We will have only half a day at school this morning.
Pupils - YAHOOO!!!
Headmaster - And we'll have the other half this afternoon.

"*How did you get on at school, Jane?*" asked her mother.
"*Today I was the best swot in the whole school, mum!*" answered Jane.
"*Really?*" said her mother.
"*Yeah. I swotted more bluebottles than anyone else!*"

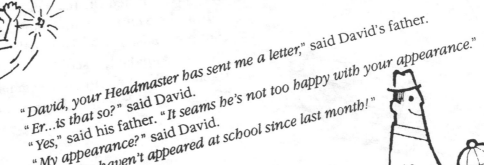

"*David, your Headmaster has sent me a letter,*" said David's father.
"*Er...is that so?*" said David.
"*Yes,*" said his father. "*It seams he's not too happy with your appearance.*"
"*My appearance?*" said David.
"*Yes. You haven't appeared at school since last month!*"

Teacher - *Give me a sentence using the word ANTENNAE.*
Pupil - *There antennae chips for lunch*

George walked into the classroom late one morning.
"*Sorry, sir,*" he said to the teacher. "*I slept in this morning.*"
"*What?*" said the teacher. "*You mean you sleep at home as well?*"

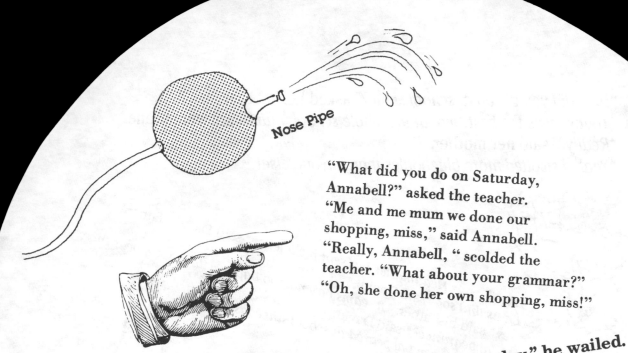

Nose Pipe

"What did you do on Saturday, Annabell?" asked the teacher.
"Me and me mum we done our shopping, miss," said Annabell.
"Really, Annabell, " scolded the teacher. "What about your grammar?"
"Oh, she done her own shopping, miss!"

"Mum, I really don't want to go to school today," he wailed.
"All the teachers hate me! All the pupils hate me!
Nobody likes me! I'm not going!"
"But you must go, dear, " said his mother.
"After all, you are the Headmaster!"

Teacher - Give me six animals you would find in Australia.
Pupil - Er... a kangaroo and five sheep!

NOSE ENTRY

Everything was quiet in the classroom. The teacher had finally got her class settled down to some work. Suddenly, someone let out an enormous burp.

"*Who did that?*" snapped the teacher.

"*Steve did, miss!*" said a tell-tale.

"*Steve,*" scolded the teacher, "*tonight I want you to stay behind and write out I must not belch in class 100 times.*"

"*But I only burped once!*" wailed Steve.

Teacher - What is the opposite of sadness?
Wally - Happiness.
Teacher - Very good. Now what is the opposite of glum?
Wally - Cheerful.
Teacher - Quite right. And the opposite of woe?
Wally - GIDDYUP!!

"*Caroline,*" said the music teacher, "*I think you should give up violin lessons and try the piano instead.*"

"*I've already tried playing the piano, miss,*" said Caroline, "*but I couldn't get it under my chin!*"

Wanda was puzzling over how to do subtraction sums correctly and her teacher decided to try to explain things simply to her.

"Look, Wanda," she said. "You have ten fingers. If you had four less what would you have?"

"No more violin lessons, miss!"

Mike was on his way home from school when he met his uncle whom he hadn't seen for ages.

"You look well, Mike," said his uncle.

"I suppose I am," agreed Mike.

"Especially since I've just had influenza, arthritis, pneumonia and eczema!"

"My goodness!" exclaimed his uncle.

"It must have been agony having all those things!"

"It sure was," replied Mike.

"Hardest spelling test I've ever had!"

Teacher - What did Sir Frances Drake say to his men before sailing off to defeat the Spanish Armada?

Pupil - Umm... all aboard!

SHOVEL

Teacher - If I put ten pound coins in my left trouser pocket and twenty pound coins in my right trouser pocket and fifty ten pence pieces in my back pocket, what would I end up with?

Pupil - Your trousers round your ankles, sir!

It was the night of the school disco and a group of parents were standing in the corner as the kids enjoyed themselves on the dance floor.

"Look at that girl over there!" gasped one stuffy woman. *"It's really not too easy to tell that she IS a girl, is it? She's wearing boy's jeans, a boy's shirt, boy's shoes and she's got a boy's haircut. Also she's not too pretty, is she?"*

"She's my daughter," was the reply.

"I'm SO sorry! " the woman apologized. *"I never realised you were her father."*

"I'm not. I'm her mother! "

"Did you have a nice lunch?" asked the teacher as her pupils filed back into the classroom after school dinner.

"Yes, miss," David replied. "I eaten seven potatoes!"

"I think you mean ate, David," said the teacher.

"NO, it was definitely seven!"

A Nose Bush

"Wash that stuff off your face at once!" yelled the teacher.
"You know that only sixth form girls are allowed to wear make-up!"
"But, miss! I'll be in the sixth form next term!"
"That will make no difference, Kevin!"

Teacher - Does anyone have any interesting hobbies
          which they do at weekends?
Pupil -   I go horseriding, sir.
Teacher - That's very interesting, Angela.
          Now, Wanda, can you tell me something
          you would find on a horse but not on any other animal?
Wanda -   Angela's bum, sir!

Tell any of these jokes at school and you'll get worse than single detention. You'll get worse than double detention. You'll get worse than than triple P.E.! You'll get quadruple school dinners! And once you've finished that you'll be taken by special puke resistant ambulance to double triple quadruple maths with all that custard you couldn't eat being forced into you on a drip feed!

Teacher - Which famous person from history said "Let them eat cake"?

Wally - Er... Mr. Kipling?

Two little girls were arguing in the
playground about how old their teacher was.
"I know how we could settle this," said one of the girls.
"How?" asked the other.
"Look in her knickers," was the reply.
"And how that help?" asked her friend.
"Well," said the first little girl,
"In my knickers it says 'Age 8 - 10'!"

Amy arrived home from school early
one afternoon. "Why are you at home
at this time?" asked her mum.
"I was sent home because the girl
next to me was smoking," said Amy.
"So why did they send you home?" her mum asked.
"It was me that set her on fire!"

On Harry's first day at play school, his mum was about to
take him along to meet all the other kids when it started snowing outside.
"Mum! Mum!" he shouted. "Can I wear my new yellow wellies?"
"Of course you can, Harry," said his mother, and off they went.
At the play school, Harry had to leave his brand new wellies in the
cloakroom and, after a hard day playing with all the other kids, it
came time to go home. While all the other kids were pulling on
their coats, the teacher found Harry sitting sobbing in the cloakroom.
"What's wrong, Harry?" she asked.
"I can't find my new yellow wellies!" howled Harry.
"Aren't these your yellow ones?" asked the teacher.
"No!" said Harry. "Mine had snow on them!"

Some jokes are so awful that you should only ever tell them while you're wearing a decent pair of trainers.

You might have to make a quick getaway! Even the worst of gags will amuse some wally somewhere, though, so here are a few just in case you are ever unlucky enough to be trapped in a lift for days on end with him. Keep him laughing and he might have second thoughts about eating you!

What do you call a woman with only one leg? *Eileen.*

What's got a wooden door and flies?
An outside toilet.

A Chinaman was suffering terrible toothache,
so he phoned up the dentist to make an appointment.
"2.30 okay?" said the dentist.
"Yeah, tooth hurty plenty!" said the Chinaman.

What wears a long coat and pants in the summer?
A dog.

After winning a million pounds on the pools a man was interviewed by a television reporter.
"Do you think that all this money will change your life?" asked the reporter.
"Certainly not!" said the man.
"And what about all the begging letters?" the reporter asked.
"Well, I'll just keep sending them!"

A little old lady was sitting by her front doorstep stroking her cat one afternoon
when the cat stood up and strolled across the road towards the park. Just then, a
car came round the corner and flattened the poor moggy.
"I'm terribly sorry," the driver said to the old lady.
"I'm afraid I've just killed your cat. I'll replace it, of course."
"Really?" said the old lady. "But can you catch mice?"

"Why did you leave your last job?" asked the employer.

"It was something my old boss said," replied the interviewee.

"What did he say?" asked the employer.

"You're sacked!"

Did you hear about the wally who went fly fishing? He caught a six pound bluebottle!

Nose Congestion

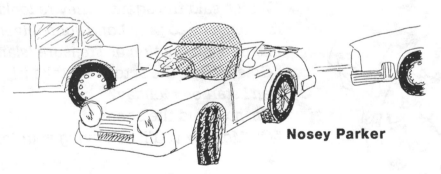

Nosey Parker

"My delivery boy sat on the bacon slicer this morning," said the grocer. "Dear me!" said the old lady. "Is he all right?" "More or less," said the grocer, "but he's got a little behind in his deliveries!"

What do men do standing up which women do sitting down and dogs do on three legs?

Shake hands!

Why did the doctor tip-toe into his medicine cupboard?
He didn't want to wake the sleeping tablets!

What do you get if you cross the Atlantic Ocean with the Titanic?.......................About half way!

An unemployed actor went to his
agent to complain about his agent
not having found him any work in months.
"*I'm getting desperate,*" said the actor.
"*I'll take anything that's going.*"
"*Well,*" said the agent, "*they're looking
for someone to play Long John Silver
in a new production of Treasure Island.*"
"*Great!*" said the actor. "*I'll take it!
Can I start on Monday?*"
"*Oh, no,*" said the agent.
"*On Monday you'll be having your leg off!*"

I CAN DO BIRD IMPRESSIONS!
I EAT WORMS!

What do Daffy and Donald like to watch on telly?
Duckumentaries!

What's the best way to keep an idiot waiting. . .

A policeman caught a well-known burglar breaking in to the back of a shop late one night.

"Aw, give's a break, guv," said the burglar. "I never get anything from you lot."

"Alright," said the policeman, "take this slip of paper."

"What's this, then?" asked the burglar.

"With that, you can get one free bash on the head," explained the policeman.

"It's a truncheon voucher!"

Johnny - What do you use to clean your front teeth with?
Joey - My toothbrush.
Johnny - And your side teeth?
Joey - The same toothbrush.
Johnny - And your bottom?
Joey - The same toothbrush.
Johnny - BLEEUCH! I use paper!

Nose Pickers

Two soldiers dived into a trench as enemy aircraft on a bombing run roared overhead.

"Blast!" said the first soldier. "I've left my false teeth behind!"

"So what?" his mate replied. "They're not dropping sandwiches, you know!"

What's the difference between lice and nits?
Nits are chewier!

. . . . I'll tell you later!

Did you hear about the Russian soldiers on parade?
The officer sneezed and six of them yelled out "Here sir!"

WHAT GOES "I'M OUT! THUD!

Hear about the Wally who burned his own ear off?
Someone phoned him while he was ironing!

Which nut invaded Britain?
William the Conker!

The actor didn't much fancy having his
leg amputated, so he asked his agent
if there were any other jobs going.
"*Hmm . . .*" said his agent. "*There's a
food company which wants someone
to dress up for an advertisement
as a giant slice of ham with cheese
and tomato between two halves
of an enormous bun.*"
"*Gee,*" said the actor.
"*Sounds like a big roll!*"

Did you hear about the workman who had a sausage stuck behind his ear?
He'd eaten his pencil for breakfast!

Did you hear about the man who went to the fancy dress party as a bone?
A dog ate him at the bus stop!

Which football players don't know each other at all?
Glasgow Strangers!

What goes "BOO-HOO! BOING! BOING!"?
Someone crying his eyes out!

Did you hear about the night hunter who
shot tigers by aiming right between their luminous eyes?
He was eaten by two one eyed tigers walking along a path arm in arm!

I divorced my wife for smoking in the toilet!
Having a cigarette in the toilet doesn't sound that bad.
Oh, she didn't smoke cigarettes - she smoked mackerel!

How do you make a rat float?

I don't know!

You take a scoop of Ice cream, a scoop of rat, add a little lemonade...

SAFE COACH

Then the actor told his agent he wanted to see
his name up in lights at the cinema.
"*In that case,*" said his agent, "*I think you'd better
change your name to TOILETS!*"

 So the actor told the agent he would
do brilliant bird impressions. *"That's no good,"* said the agent.
"Bird impressions aren't different enough."
"Suit yourself," said the actor and flew off out the window.

What's small and green and eats pebbles.
A small green pebble eater!

WHAT ROARS ALONG YOUR WASHING LINE AT 100MPH?

Woman - I need a mousetrap, quick. I've got a bus to catch.
Shopkeeper - Sorry, madam, we don't make them that big!

What's yellow and white and goes from London to Birmingham at

I got fifty Valentine cards last year.
I was too shy to post them, though!

What do you call a girl who carries
an encyclopedia in her knickers?
Smarty Pants!

**What must you be careful
of when it's raining cats and dogs?
Not to step in a poodle!**

HONDA PANTS!

A cowboy was out on the range when he
came across an Indian with his ear
pressed down hard against the trail.
"What you doin' down there, pardner?" he asked.
"Stagecoach pass this way
half an hour ago,"
said the Indian.
"How can you tell that?"
asked the cowboy.
"IT RAN OVER MY HEAD!!"

I Say! I Say! I Say! What's red and lumpy, wears a mask
and rides a horse through the desert? The Lone Raspberry!

Why was the beach all wet?
The sea weed.

25mph? The train driver's egg sandwich!

Did you hear about the plastic surgeon
warming himself by the fire?
He melted!

A con man was arrested and brought in to the police station.
"*All right*," said the desk sergeant. "*What's your name?*"
"*John Smith*," said the con man.
"*Don't give me that*," warned the sergeant.
"*I want your real name.*"
"*Okay*," said the con man. "*Napoleon Bonaparte.*"
"*That's better*," said the sergeant.
"*You can't fool me with all that John Smith nonsense!*"

Right! Has anyone seen that puppy?

ANGEL AD–MEN MAKING HEAVEN'S
FIRST ANDREX COMMERCIAL

What do you call a man with a car on his head? Jack!

What did the salad cream say in the fridge?
Close the door, I'm dressing!

**The Great Supremo was trying to attract customers to his stall at the funfair.
"I'll answer any question for five pounds!" he called.
"That's a bit dear, isn't it? said a passer by.
"Yes!" cried the Great Supremo.
"That'll be five pounds, please!"**

Three men were sentenced to death during the French revolution. One of them was a real wally, so the others didn't let him in on their plan. They had bribed the executioner to jam a wooden peg in the side of the guillotine to stop the blade from falling all the way down.

When the first of them was brought to be executed, he placed his neck on the block and the executioner pulled the handle to release the blade. As planned, the blade stuck halfway down.

"Since the guillotine has not worked," announced the executioner, "this man must go free!"

When the second prisoner was brought out, he placed his head on the block and exactly the same thing happened.

"Since the guillotine has not worked," announced the executioner, "this man must go free!"

Next, they brought out the wally who placed his head on the block but, being a wally, he did it the wrong way, facing upwards instead of downwards. Then, just as the executioner was about to pull the handle he yelled out:

"Wait a minute! I see what's sticking it!"

The hotel lift boy was showing off in
his new high speed lift when a lady guest got in.
"*Take me up to the twentieth floor, quickly,*" she said.
The lift boy pushed the button for the twentieth floor
and the button for full speed.
"*That too quick for you?*" he asked when they arrived three seconds later.
"*No,*" said the woman. "*I always wear my knickers round my ankles.*"

War of the Noses

Policeman - Caught you red handed again, Napper.
Why do you always insist on burgling only second floor flats?
Burglar - Well, that's my storey and I'm sticking to it!

What do you get if you cross a
carpet with an elephant?
A deep pile in your living room!

What's the difference between dogs and fleas?
A dog can have fleas but a flea can't have dogs!

Where do pixies and elves go shopping?
British Gnome Stores and Littleweeds!

Eventually the actor got a part in Lassie.
He played the lead!

Even the most brilliant pair of trainers in the entire universe won't get you out of trouble quickly enough if you start telling any of these gags. People will stuff cushions, pillows, quilts or even entire carpets in your mouth to shut you up. They'll throw anything handy at you - a brick, a lampost, a piano, an armadillo. A suit of armour and a motorbike might be more use than a pair of trainers! So, if you ever see anyone roaring along the street on a motorbike wearing a suit of armour with a carpet in his mouth and being pelted with armadillos, you'll know what he's been up to . . .

**How do you get paper babies?
Marry an old bag!**

**Why was the bank clerk sitting up a tree?
He wanted to be a branch manager!**

*"Scuse me, missus," said the bus conductor, "but did you know
that you have a banana in your ear?"
"Sorry," said the woman. "I can't hear you.
I've got a banana in my ear!"*

Why is an elephant big and grey and wrinkly?
Because if it was small and white and smooth it would be an aspirin!

**How can you tell when a motorcyclist has been
having fun speeding on the motorway?
By all the flies in his teeth.**

Knock!Knock! jokes are okay in small doses - like one every second leap year. Choose your Knock!Knock! jokes with great care and use them sparingly otherwise your friends will lay land mines in the garden path when they know you're coming or train sabre-toothed ninja attack sparrows. And watch out for cunningly disguised snipers.

Knock knock!
Who's there?
Wendy.
Wendy who?
Wendy bell break, then!

Knock knock! Who's there? Yah. Yah who? Calm down, you nutter!

Knock knock!
Who's there?
Esther.
Esther who?
Esther rent man! Open up!

Knock knock!
Who's there?
Kent.
Kent who?
Kent you guess?

Knock knock! Who's there?
Cecily. Cecily who?
Cecily question, isn't it?

Knock knock!
Who's there?
Sarah.
Sarah who?
Sarah any way to get you to open up?

Knock knock!
Who's there?
Pedro.
Pedro who?
Pedro Poll Tax yet?

Knock knock! Who's there? Phyllis. Phyllis who? Phyllis bucket and I'll clean your windows.

Knock knock! -Who's there? -Alec. -Alec who? Alectricity man. I've come to read the meter!

KNOCK KNOCK!
Who's there?
IZZY.
Izzy who?
IZZY ANYBODY IN?

Киоск! Киоск!
Щно's Тнеяе?
Ivaи.
Ivaи Щно?
Ivaи то соме iи!

Лтщсл Лтщсл1
Цpщы еpукуЁ
Шмфтю
Шмфт цpщЁ
Шмфт ещ сщьу шт1

Knock knock!
Who's there?
Waddle.
Waddle who?
Waddle it take to get you to let me in?

Knock knock!
Who's there?
Isabel.
Isabel who?
Isabel broken, or what?

Knock knock!
Who's there?
Auntie.
Auntie who?
Auntie gonna open the door yet?

KNOCK KNOCK!
Who's there?
LIONEL.
Lionel who?
LIONEL NOT WORK! I KNOW YOU'RE IN THERE!

Knock knock! Who's there? Wanda. Wanda who?
Wanda let me in? It's freezing out here!

Knock knock! Who's there? Howard. Howard who?
Howard you expect to find out, if you don't open up!

Knock knock!
Who's there?
Cynthia.
Cynthia.
Cynthia who?
Cynthia four jokes like this so far!

KNOCK KNOCK! WHO'S THERE? DORIS. DORIS WHO?
DORIS STILL SHUT AND I'M STILL FREEZING OUT HERE!

Knock knock!
Who's there?
Ewan.
Ewan who?
No, just me!

Knock knock!
Who's there?
Just Colin.
Just Colin who?
Just Colin round for that fiver you owe me!

Knock knock!
Who's there?
Olive.
Olive who?
Olive here too, don't I?

Knock knock!
Who's there?
Trish.
Trish who?
That's a nasty cold you've got!

KNOCK KNOCK!
WHO'S THERE?
DAWN.
DAWN WHO?
DAWN LEAVE ME OUT HERE!

Knock knock!
Who's there?
Rosa.
Rosa who?
Rosa people out here waiting to get in!

Knock knock!
Who's there?
Twit.
Twit who?
You got an *owl* in there?

Knock knock!
Who's there?
Owls.
Owls who?
Yes, they do, don't they

KNOCK KNOCK! WHO'S THERE? IVAN. IVAN WHO?
IVAN IDEA YOU'RE NOT GOING TO LET ME IN!

Knock knock! Who's there? Sis. Sis who?
SIS THE MILLIONTH "KNOCK KNOCK!" JOKE I'VE TOLD!

Knock knock! Who's there?
Mickey. *Mickey who?*
Mickey's stuck in the lock!

Knock knock! *Who's there?* Adolf. *Adolf who?*
A dolf ball hit me in the mouf fo now I fpeak funny!

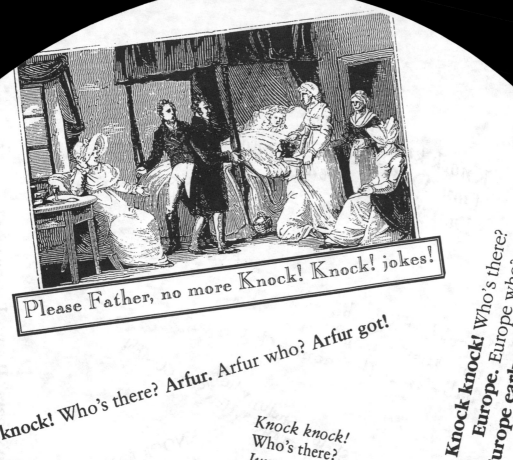

Please Father, no more Knock! Knock! jokes!

Knock knock! Who's there? Arfur. Arfur who? Arfur got!

Knock knock!
Who's there?
Juno.
Juno who?
'Course I do!

Knock knock!
Who's there?
Amy.
Amy who?
Amy fraid I've forgotten!

Knock knock! Who's there?
Europe. Europe who?
Europe early this morning!

Knock knock!
Who's there?
Des.
Des who?
Des no bell out here is there?

KNOCK KNOCK!
WHO'S THERE?
POLICE.
POLICE WHO?
POLICE LET ME IN, I'M LONELY!

Knock knock! Who's there?
Don. Don who?
Don you ever open this door?

Knock knock!
Who's there?
Ken.
Ken who?
Ken I come in, please?

Knock knock! Who's there?
Justin. Justin who?
Justin the hallway at the moment!

Knock knock! -Who's there? -Shelby. -Shelby who?
SHELBY COMING ROUND THE MOUNTAINS WHEN SHE COMES!

KNOCK KNOCK!
WHO'S THERE?
WELCOME.
WELCOME WHO?
WELCOME ON, OPEN UP!

Knock knock! Who's there? Donna. Donna who?
Donna wanna here any more of these stupid jokes!!!

Knock knock!
Who's there?
Wayne.
Wayne who?
Wayne you gonna open up?

On no account EVER
tell these Knock knock!
jokes at anyone's front door.
Not only will you be left
standing in the cold, 596
gallons of specially prepared
lumpy semolina garnished
liberally with dead dogs and
donkey droppings will
cascade down on you from
a secret overhead
trapdoor.
You have been warned.

Knock knock! Who's there?
Sal. *Sal who?*
Salong way to Tipperary . . .

Knock knock!
Who's there?
Nettie.
Nettie who?
Nettie bell here then?

Knock knock! Who's there? Butcher. Butcher who?
Butcher left leg in, your left leg out . . .

Knock knock! Who's there? Dunap. Dunap who?
What, right there on the carpet?

Knock knock!
Who's there?
Hank.
Hank who?
You're welcome!

Knock knock! Who's there? Carrie. Carrie who?
Carrie me across the threshold, darling!

Knock knock!
Who's there?
Nick.
Nick who?
Nicker elastic's burst! Let me in!

SHOVEL

Comic Relief is now in its fifth year, and our serious commitment to the work we support grows – as, unfortunately, does the need for that work.

AFRICA

We are still passionately committed to our work in Africa, where over the past years we've made 282 grants in 29 countries in support of both long term development and emergency work.

Long Term Development

We've given grants to...
Farmers in Ethiopia, health-workers to remove Guinea Worm in Burkina Faso, orphans in Mozambique, wells in Uganda, teachers in Kenya, health services in Somalia, schools in Sudan, carpenters in Zimbabwe and hundreds of others.

Emergency

Comic Relief was set up primarily in reaction to the famine in 1984. Food shortages now loom in the horn of Africa again, and we will continue to support emergency operations.

THE UK

We don't just help people in Africa. There are also serious problems in the UK. Over the past years we've made well over 1000 grants to organisations all over the UK, some probably just round the corner from you. We've split our help into four areas of concern:

Homelessness – This is a real crisis area where young lives can be ruined in a matter of weeks. We try to tackle the problem at all ends – to prevent young people ending up on the streets, to provide a roof over their heads, and to search for long-term solutions.

Drug and Alcohol Misuse – We help young people in trouble and we also try to stop drugs and alcohol ever taking a grip.

Disability – We're working with lots of groups involving young people with disabilities fighting for independence, integration and rights.

Older People – Up and down the country, we are helping pensioners who are working to help themselves, to draw attention to their needs and improve their rights.

WE CAN'T CHANGE THE PROBLEMS OF THE WORLD, BUT WHAT RED NOSE DAY GIVES EVERYONE AT COMIC RELIEF AND ALL ITS SUPPORTERS IS AN OPPORTUNITY TO REACH OUT TO OTHER PEOPLE WITH THE MONEY THEY NEED TO RADICALLY CHANGE THEIR LIVES.

And remember...

All of the money sent to Comic Relief will go straight to support charitable projects in Africa and the UK. None of it goes on salaries or administration because all of that is covered by sponsorship or by the interest on banked money.